Agile Scrum
Dynamics

MOHAMED FAWZI ELGENDI
WWW.FAWZOOZ.AI

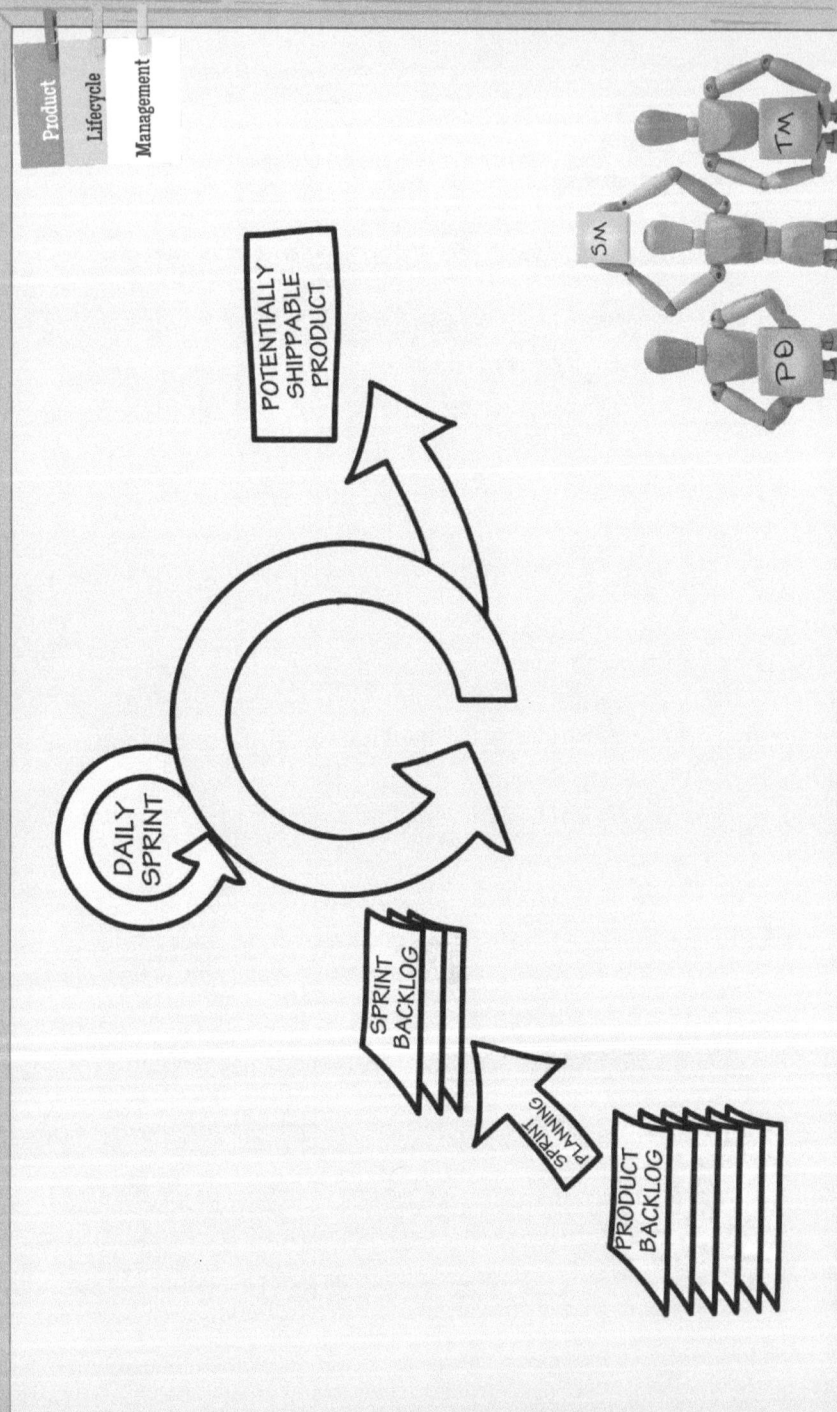

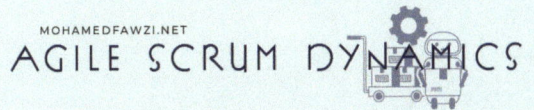

Copyright © 2024 Mohamed Fawzi Elgendi

No part of this work may be reproduced, distributed, transmitted in any form or by any means, including photocopying, recording, or other electronic or mechanical methods, without the prior written permission of the author, except in the case of brief quotations embodied in critical reviews and certain other noncommercial uses permitted by copyright law with the source duly credited. The names, characters, businesses, places, events, locales, and incidents are either the products of the author's imagination or used in a fictitious manner. Any resemblance to actual persons, living or dead, or actual events is purely coincidental. www.mohamedfawzi.net

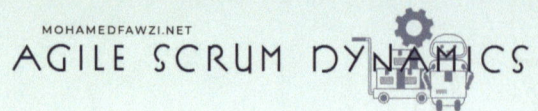

Table of Contents

Preface 6

Introduction to Scrum in Creative Fields 10

Adapting Scrum for Creative Teams 17

Key Practices in Scrum for Creative Teams 23

Tools and Technologies for Creative Scrum Teams 30

Implementing Scrum in Creative Teams 35

Advanced Scrum Techniques for Creative Teams 41

The Future of Scrum in Creative Fields 47

Bringing It All Together 53

Conclusion 60

Comprehensive Case Study 64

ABOUT THE AUTHOR 71

2024

PREFACE

WWW.MOHAMEDFAWZI.NET

AGILE SCRUM
DYNAMICS

Preface

Welcome to "Agile Scrum Dynamics", a book where tradition meets innovation in the realm of project management and productivity enhancement. This guide is designed for creative professionals, team leaders, and anyone intrigued by the potential of Scrum to transform traditional workflows into dynamic, collaborative, and adaptive processes. Here, we will embark on a journey to discover how the Scrum framework, originally developed for software development, can be just as revolutionary in marketing, design, media production, and more.

The genesis of this book lies in the realization that while Scrum has been extensively documented and explored within technical fields, there is a burgeoning opportunity to adapt its principles to the creative sectors that thrive on flexibility, innovation, and speed. The goal of this book is not merely to

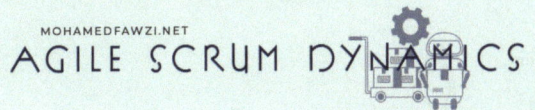

transplant a methodology from one discipline to another but to translate and tailor its essence for the unique challenges and opportunities found in creative environments.

Why Scrum for Creatives?

The fast-paced nature of creative work, with its need for constant innovation and adaptation, mirrors the ever-evolving landscape of technology development. Scrum's emphasis on iterative progress, team collaboration, and rapid response to change aligns perfectly with the goals of creative teams—from graphic designers brainstorming for a campaign to event managers coordinating large-scale projects.

In this book, you will find a detailed exploration of Scrum basics reinterpreted for the creative industries. You will learn how to apply these practices to foster a collaborative team environment where innovative ideas are realized swiftly and efficiently. Through real-world examples, practical advice, and

step-by-step guides, we will examine how Scrum can enhance not just productivity but also the creative quality of outputs.

Navigating the Book

The structure of this book is designed to guide you from the fundamentals of Scrum through its implementation in creative projects, and into advanced techniques for mastering and scaling these practices. Whether you are new to Scrum or seeking to refine your existing knowledge with a creative twist, this book aims to be a valuable resource.

As we delve into these pages, I encourage you to think of Scrum not just as a methodology, but as a mindset—one that emphasizes communication, collaboration, and continuous improvement.

Let's begin this transformative journey, and unlock new levels of creativity and efficiency in your projects.

Chapter 1
Introduction to Scrum in Creative Fields

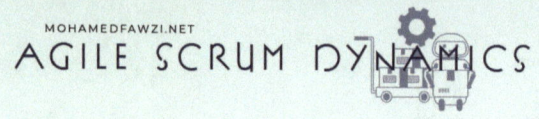

Chapter 1

Introduction to Scrum in Creative Fields

Scrum is a framework used to support complex project management, traditionally in software development but increasingly in other fields. It helps teams address complex problems while productively and creatively delivering products of the highest possible value. Scrum is not a process, technique, or definitive method. Instead, it is a framework within which you can employ various processes and techniques.

The Origins of Scrum

Scrum was formalized for software development projects in the early 1990s, derived from work by Hirotaka Takeuchi and Ikujiro Nonaka in their 1986 Harvard Business Review article, "The New

New Product Development Game". They introduced a holistic approach to product development that increases speed and flexibility by using small, cross-functional teams. This approach has since been adapted across different industries, proving particularly beneficial where innovation is the key to success.

Scrum Basics

At its core, Scrum involves a small team led by a Scrum Master, who champions the project, facilitating the process and protecting the team from outside distractions. Key roles include:

- **The Product Owner**: Responsible for maximizing the value of the product resulting from the work of the Scrum Team.

- **The Development Team**: Professionals who deliver the product (a potentially releasable increment of "Done" product at the end of each Sprint).

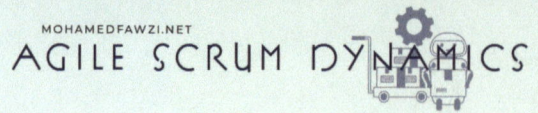

Scrum Artifacts:

- **Product Backlog**: An ordered list of everything that is needed in the product.

- **Sprint Backlog**: Set of Product Backlog items selected for the Sprint, plus a plan for delivering the product Increment and realizing the Sprint Goal.

- **Increment**: The sum of all the Product Backlog items completed during a Sprint and the value of the increments of all previous Sprints.

Scrum Events:

- **Sprint**: A time-box of one month or less during which a "Done", useable, and potentially releasable product Increment is created.

- **Sprint Planning**: Event marking the start of the Sprint.

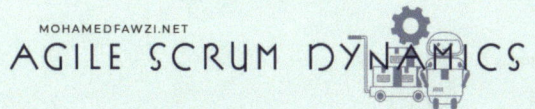

- **Daily Scrum**: 15-minute event for the Development Team to synchronize activities and create a plan for the next 24 hours.

- **Sprint Review**: Held at the end of the Sprint to inspect the Increment and adapt the Product Backlog if needed.

- **Sprint Retrospective**: An opportunity for the Scrum Team to inspect itself and create a plan for improvements to be enacted during the next Sprint.

Adapting Scrum to Creative Projects

While Scrum's origins are in software, its principles are highly adaptable to creative projects. For example, in advertising, the increment could be draft designs or campaign ideas. In event planning, it might be the layout and vendor list. The adaptability of Scrum lies in its simplicity and the focus on iterative progress, transparency, and team collaboration.

Benefits of Scrum in Creative Environments

- **Flexibility and Responsiveness**: Creative projects often experience frequent changes. Scrum allows teams to adapt quickly and respond to feedback and changes in client needs or market conditions.

- **Enhanced Collaboration**: By working in short sprints and having regular touchpoints (Daily Scrums), teams maintain a high level of communication and can align more closely on project goals and adjustments.

- **Increased Productivity**: By focusing on small increments of work, teams can focus their efforts more effectively, leading to higher productivity and better use of resources.

- **Continuous Improvement**: Through regular retrospectives, teams continually refine their processes, leading to improvements in efficiency and output over time.

This introduction to Scrum provides a solid foundation for understanding how it can be adapted to facilitate innovation and manage projects in creative fields. As we explore further, the following chapters will delve into practical applications, helping you to tailor the Scrum framework to fit the unique needs of your creative projects.

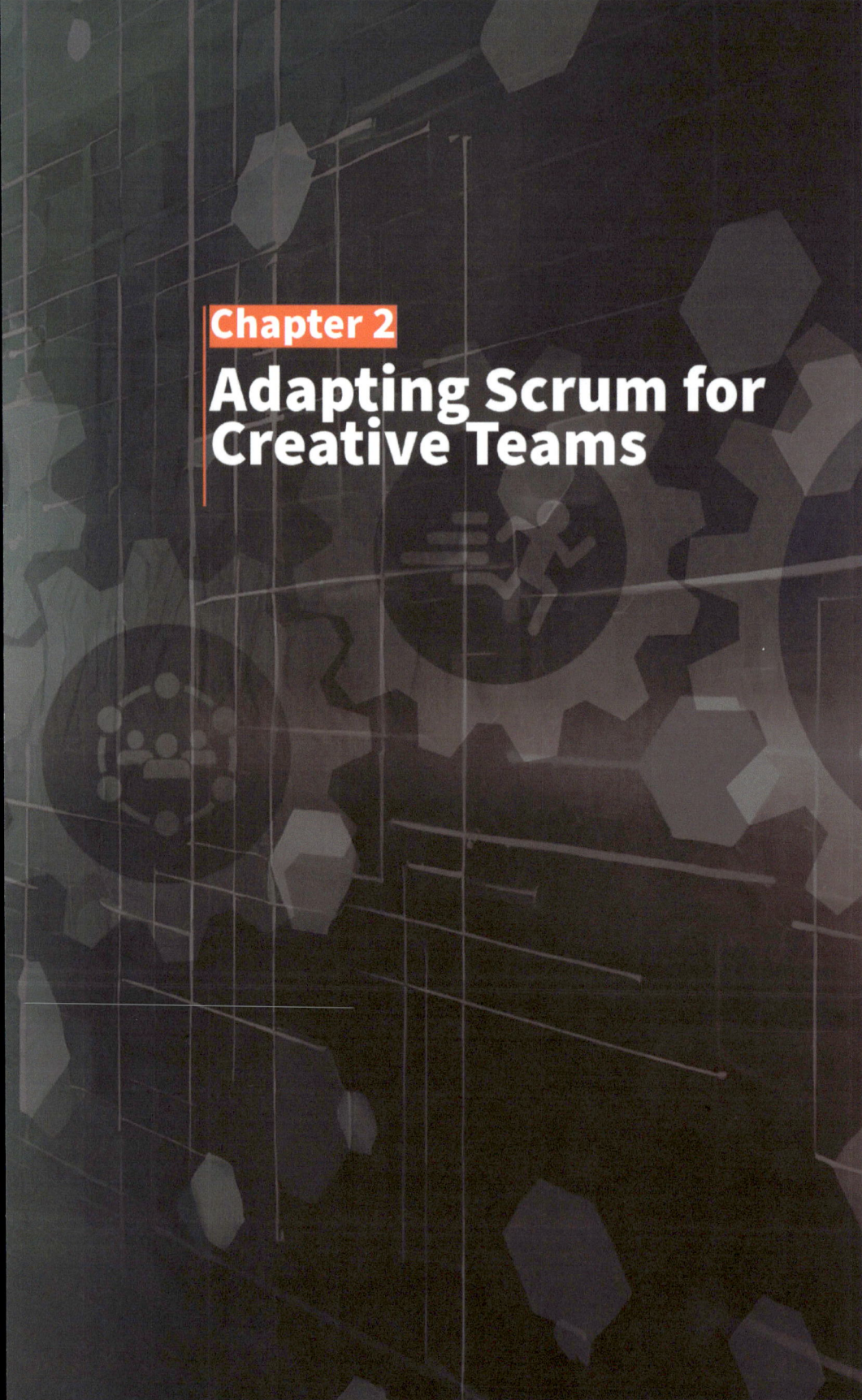
Chapter 2
Adapting Scrum for Creative Teams

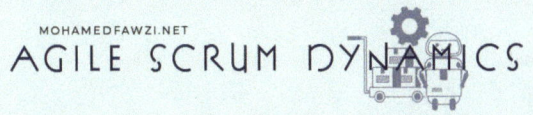

Chapter 2

Adapting Scrum for Creative Teams

While Scrum is traditionally associated with software development, its principles are universally applicable and can profoundly impact creative fields. This chapter explores how to adapt the structured world of Scrum to the fluid and often unpredictable nature of creative projects.

Scrum for Creatives

1. **Roles Redefined**:

   - **Product Owner**: In creative projects, this role might be akin to a Creative Director or Project Lead, responsible for

maintaining the project's vision and ensuring that the final deliverables align with client expectations and business goals.

   - **Scrum Master**: Acts as a facilitator and coach, ensuring that the creative team remains unfettered by internal and external distractions. This role could be filled by a senior team member who has a deep understanding of both creative work and agile practices.

   - **Development Team**: Comprises designers, writers, artists, and other creative professionals who work collaboratively to develop and deliver the project's creative elements.

2. **Customizing Scrum Artifacts**:

   - **Product Backlog**: For creative projects, this might include a mix of creative deliverables, concept revisions, client feedback sessions, and other elements needed to complete the project.

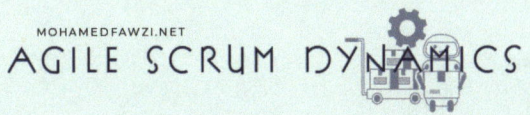

  - **Sprint Backlog**: Adapted to include creative tasks that have been broken down into manageable actions that can be completed within a sprint, allowing for regular review and adaptation.

  - **Increment:** Defined as a usable and potentially releasable state of creative work at the end of each sprint, which could be a campaign prototype, a series of design layouts, or a section of completed video.

3. **Modifying Scrum Events:**

  - **Sprint Planning**: Involves collaborative session where creative teams decide on the deliverables for the upcoming sprint, basing decisions on client needs, creative inspiration, and project timelines.

  - **Daily Scrum**: A short daily meeting where the team discusses progress and roadblocks, particularly useful in creative projects for synchronizing creative ideas and ensuring consistency.

- **Sprint Review**: A showcase of creative work completed during the sprint to stakeholders and clients for feedback.

- **Sprint Retrospective**: Focuses on evaluating the creative process, discussing what worked well and what didn't, and making adjustments to improve creativity and productivity.

Practical Tips for Implementing Scrum in Creative Environments

1. **Foster a Collaborative Culture**: Encourage open communication and collective decision-making to make the most of the diverse creative talents on your team.

2. **Embrace Flexibility in Processes**: While Scrum emphasizes structure, adapt its ceremonies and artifacts to the fluid nature of creative work where requirements can change rapidly.

3. **Visualize Workflows**: Use tools like Kanban boards or digital project management tools to visualize tasks and workflows,

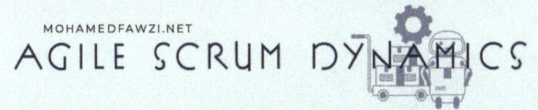

which can help creative teams see their progress and plan more effectively.

4. **Iterative Development**: Focus on building creative concepts and campaigns incrementally. This approach allows for testing and refinement, ensuring that the end product truly resonates with the target audience.

5. **Continuous Feedback Loops**: Incorporate regular feedback sessions not only from clients but also from other stakeholders and team members to enhance the creative output and ensure alignment with the project goals.

Adapting Scrum to creative projects involves more than just implementing a new process; it requires a shift in mindset. By redefining roles, customizing Scrum artifacts, and modifying its events, creative teams can harness the structure of Scrum to unleash their creativity more effectively and efficiently.

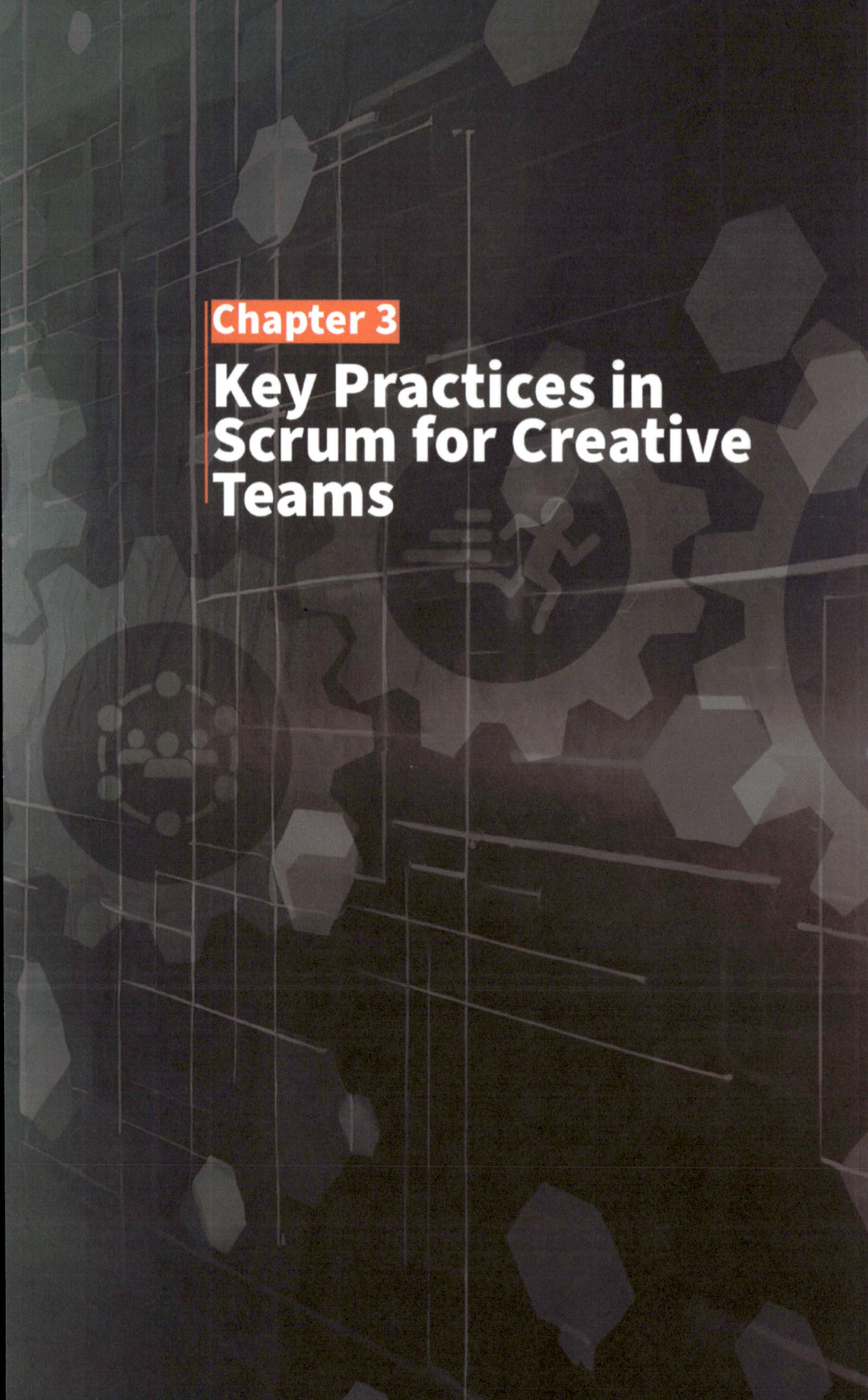

Chapter 3
Key Practices in Scrum for Creative Teams

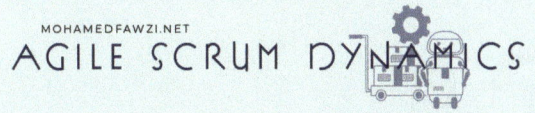

Chapter 3

Key Practices in Scrum for Creative Teams

Having adapted the roles and processes of Scrum to fit creative environments, it is crucial to implement key practices that support these adaptations. This chapter focuses on practical Scrum practices that are essential for ensuring creative projects are not only innovative but also delivered efficiently and effectively.

Secure Coding Practices for Creative Teams

While "coding" might not always be literal in creative fields, the concept of "coding" can be thought of as setting up standardized procedures or templates which ensure quality and

consistency in creative outputs, such as design elements or marketing copy.

1. **Standardization of Creative Assets:**

 - Establishing guidelines for design elements ensures consistency across a project.

 - Using templates and predefined assets speeds up the creative process while maintaining high standards.

2. **Version Control for Creative Content:**

 - Utilizing tools like Git for design projects (with platforms such as GitHub or Bitbucket) to manage changes and revisions efficiently.

 - Ensuring all team members can revert to previous versions or explore alternate designs without losing progress.

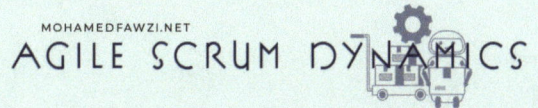

Automated Security Testing in Creative Workflows

Automation in creative projects often involves automating repetitive tasks to allow creatives more time to focus on innovation and design.

1. **Automation Tools:**

   - Using software like Adobe's Creative Cloud Libraries to automate asset sharing and updates across teams.

   - Implementing project management tools that automate workflow processes and reminders.

2. **Integration into Creative Software:**

   - Plugins for design software that automate formatting, asset optimization, and preliminary quality checks.

Threat Modeling and Risk Assessment for Creative Projects

Identifying potential project risks and preparing for them is crucial to ensure that creative projects meet deadlines and quality standards without exceeding budget.

1. **Risk Identification in Creative Planning**:

   - Early identification of potential bottlenecks in creative projects, such as key approval stages or dependency on specific resources.

   - Regular risk assessment meetings to adjust timelines and resources as projects progress.

2. **Proactive Solutions**:

   - Establishing contingency plans for key risks, such as alternate sourcing for materials or additional staffing solutions.

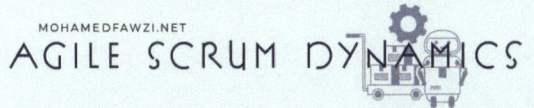

- Using historical data from previous projects to predict and mitigate potential delays or challenges.

Implementing Continuous Monitoring and Feedback

Continuous monitoring and the implementation of feedback mechanisms are vital to keeping creative projects on track and aligned with client expectations.

1. **Real-Time Progress Tracking**:

   - Utilizing dashboards that provide at-a-glance views of project statuses and milestones.

   - Daily or weekly check-ins to monitor progress and address any issues promptly.

2. **Feedback Loops**:

   - Structured feedback sessions during and after each sprint to gather insights from all stakeholders.

   - Incorporating feedback into the creative process to refine and improve outputs continually.

Implementing these key Scrum practices in creative fields ensures that projects are not only completed efficiently but also meet the high standards expected in creative outputs. This chapter has outlined specific techniques and tools that can be used to embed these practices into the daily workflow of creative teams, enhancing their productivity and the quality of their creative projects.

Chapter 4
Tools and Technologies for Creative Scrum

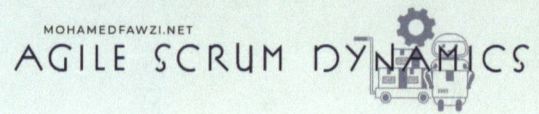

Chapter 4

Tools and Technologies for Creative Scrum Teams

Integrating the right tools and technologies is essential for creative Scrum teams to maximize their productivity and creativity. This chapter explores various types of tools that support Scrum practices and enhance collaboration and efficiency in creative environments.

Essential Tools for Creative Scrum Teams

1. **Project Management Tools**:

   - These tools should support visual task management, progress tracking, and real-time collaboration, enabling teams to manage Scrum boards and sprints effectively.

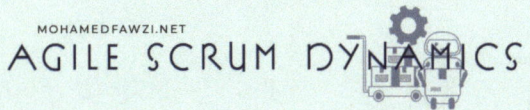

2. **Communication Tools**:

   - Platforms that facilitate instant messaging, video calls, and file sharing are vital for ensuring continuous communication, particularly in teams that may include remote members.

3. **Design and Development Collaboration Tools:**

   - Tools that enable design prototyping, feedback collection, and version control are crucial for creative teams. They allow for rapid iteration and effective incorporation of feedback.

4. **Version Control Systems:**

   - Essential for teams working with digital creations, these systems help manage changes to documents and other files, facilitating collaboration and preventing conflicts.

5. **Documentation and Asset Management:**

- Solutions that help organize and store project documentation, creative assets, and collaborative notes are key to keeping materials accessible and well-organized.

Integrating Tools into the Scrum Workflow

Choosing the Right Tools:

- Evaluate the specific needs of your project and team to select tools that will effectively support your objectives. Consider factors such as scalability, integration capabilities, and user-friendliness.

Setting Up for Efficiency:

- Ensure that the selected tools are well integrated, facilitating seamless workflows and information sharing.

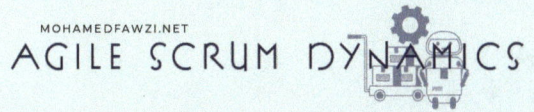

- Configure notifications and automations to streamline tasks and keep the team focused on creative outputs.

Training and Adoption:

- Provide training to ensure all team members are proficient with the new tools.

- Encourage ongoing feedback on the tools' effectiveness and usability, and be prepared to make adjustments based on team input.

The right set of tools can significantly enhance the effectiveness of Scrum in creative projects. By carefully selecting and integrating these technologies into your Scrum workflow, you can enhance collaboration, streamline communication, and boost overall productivity. This enables your team to deliver high-quality creative content more efficiently, fully embracing the agile principles of Scrum.

Chapter 5
Implementing Scrum in Creative Teams

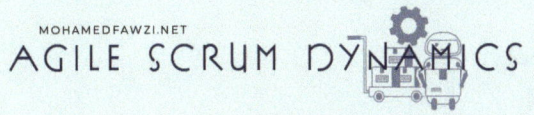

Chapter 5

Implementing Scrum in Creative Teams

Transitioning to Scrum in creative teams requires careful planning and execution. This chapter outlines a step-by-step approach to successfully implement Scrum, focusing on practical strategies to adapt Scrum principles to fit the unique needs of creative projects.

Step-by-Step Guide to Scrum Implementation

1. **Initial Assessment and Planning:**

   - **Evaluate Current Workflows**: Assess existing project management practices to identify what works and what needs improvement.

- **Define Goals and Objectives**: Clearly outline what you aim to achieve with Scrum, such as faster turnaround times, improved team collaboration, or enhanced project flexibility.

2. **Agile Scrum Dynamics**

- **Customize Scrum Roles:** Adapt the roles of Product Owner, Scrum Master, and Development Team to fit the creative context, assigning responsibilities that align with creative workflows.

- **Develop Scrum Artifacts:** Tailor artifacts like the Product Backlog, Sprint Backlog, and Increment to suit creative outputs, such as design drafts, content pieces, and campaign elements.

3. **Training and Team Onboarding:**

- **Conduct Scrum Workshops:** Organize workshops to educate the team on Scrum principles, roles, events, and artifacts.

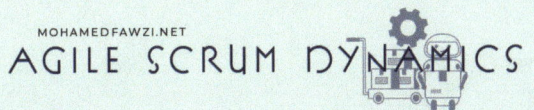

- **Role-Specific Training:** Provide detailed training for each Scrum role, focusing on the specific responsibilities and expectations in the creative context.

4. **Implementing Scrum Events:**

- **Sprint Planning:** Guide teams on how to plan sprints effectively, focusing on setting realistic goals for creative outputs.

- **Daily Scrum:** Introduce daily stand-up meetings to keep the team aligned and address any immediate hurdles.

- **Sprint Review and Retrospective:** Implement these meetings to review completed work and discuss ways to improve processes in future sprints.

5. **Iterative Refinement and Scaling:**

  - **Review and Adapt**: Regularly assess the effectiveness of Scrum practices and make adjustments based on team feedback and project outcomes.

  - **Scale Scrum Practices**: Explore ways to expand Scrum practices as the team grows or as projects increase in complexity.

Overcoming Common Challenges

- **Resistance to Change**: Manage skepticism and resistance by clearly communicating the benefits of Scrum and involving the team in the transition process.

- **Maintaining Creativity**: Address concerns about the structured nature of Scrum potentially stifling creativity by ensuring flexibility in how tasks and projects are managed.

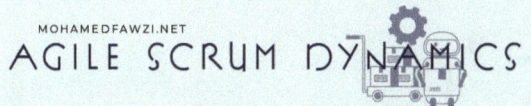

- **Balancing Flexibility and Structure**: Find the right balance between the structured Scrum framework and the inherent need for flexibility in creative processes.

Implementing Scrum in a creative environment can transform how teams approach project management, enhancing their ability to produce high-quality creative work efficiently. By following the outlined steps and continuously adapting to the team's needs, creative teams can fully leverage the benefits of Scrum to achieve their project goals.

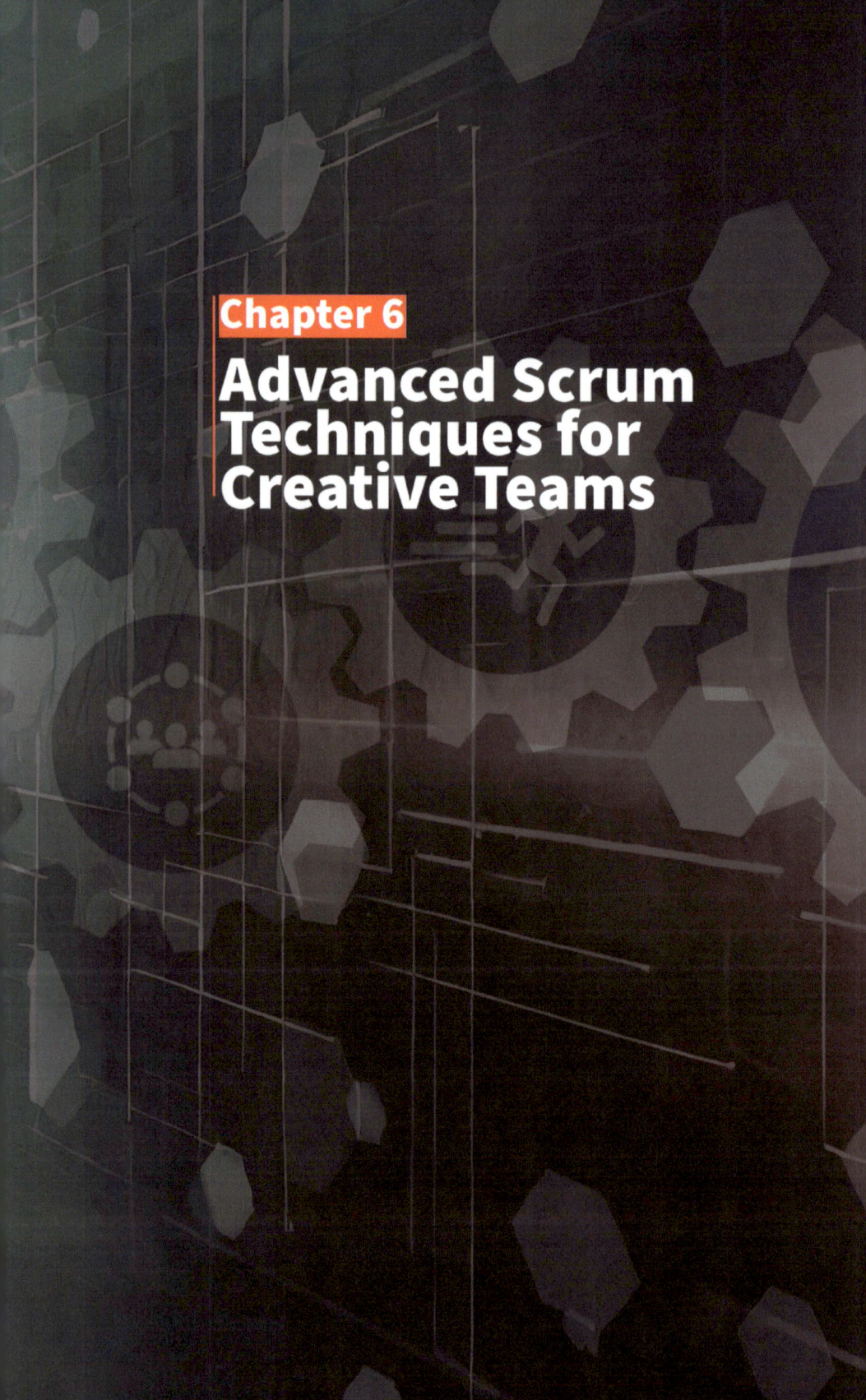

Chapter 6
Advanced Scrum Techniques for Creative Teams

Chapter 6

Advanced Scrum Techniques for Creative Teams

Once a creative team has successfully implemented Scrum and adapted it to their workflow, the next step is to refine and optimize these practices. This chapter introduces advanced techniques that can help creative teams maximize the benefits of Scrum, fostering continuous improvement and innovation.

Advanced Scrum Techniques

1. **Enhancing Collaboration Through Technology:**

   - Explore tools and platforms that enhance collaboration, especially for teams that include remote members or work

across different time zones. Focus on technologies that facilitate seamless communication and real-time feedback.

2. **Implementing Scrum at Scale:**

   - Discuss strategies for scaling Scrum in larger organizations or across multiple creative departments. This includes integrating various Scrum teams within an organization to work cohesively while maintaining the flexibility and autonomy of individual teams.

3. **Customizing Scrum Ceremonies for Creativity:**

   - Tailor Scrum events to better suit creative processes. For instance, modify the Sprint Review to showcase creative work in a more interactive and engaging way that solicits more constructive feedback.

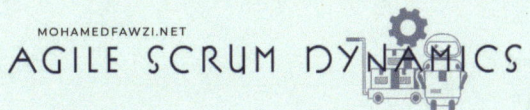

4. **Using Metrics to Drive Improvement:**

  - Identify and implement key performance indicators (KPIs) that are relevant to creative projects. Use these metrics to track progress, measure effectiveness, and guide decision-making processes within the team.

5. **Incorporating Design Thinking into Scrum:**

  - Merge principles of design thinking with Scrum practices to enhance problem-solving and innovation within the team. This can involve rethinking problem identification, ideation, and rapid prototyping within Sprints.

Techniques for Sustaining Scrum Practices

1. **Continuous Learning and Adaptation:**

  - Encourage ongoing education and training to keep up with the latest Scrum methodologies and tools. Foster a culture of

learning where team members are encouraged to bring new ideas and techniques to improve the Scrum process.

2. **Building a Feedback-Rich Environment:**

   - Develop mechanisms for continuous feedback, not just from clients but also internally among team members. Use these insights to refine workflows, improve collaboration, and enhance the overall creative output.

3. **Fostering Team Autonomy and Ownership:**

   - Empower teams by giving them more control over their work and the decision-making process within the Scrum framework. This can increase motivation and encourage more innovative solutions to emerge from the team.

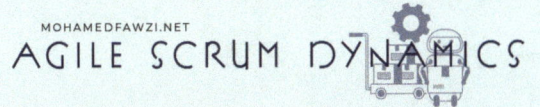

Overcoming Advanced Challenges

- **Complexity in Coordination:** As projects and teams grow, maintaining effective coordination can become challenging. Implement advanced Scrum tools and techniques specifically designed to handle complex project management scenarios.

- **Innovation Stagnation**: Address the risk of routine setting in, which can stifle creativity. Regularly refresh and revise Scrum practices to keep the team's approach innovative and dynamic.

Advanced Scrum techniques offer a pathway to not only sustain but also enhance the creative capabilities of teams. By continuously refining these practices and integrating new strategies, teams can maintain a high level of productivity and innovation, ensuring that Scrum remains an effective tool for managing creative projects.

Chapter 7
The Future of Scrum in Creative Fields

Chapter 7

The Future of Scrum in Creative Fields

As industries continue to evolve with advances in technology and changes in consumer behavior, the application of Scrum in creative fields must also adapt. This chapter discusses the future directions of Scrum, highlighting emerging trends, potential challenges, and how creative teams can stay ahead of the curve.

Emerging Trends in Scrum for Creative Teams

1. **Integration of AI and Automation:**

   - Explore how artificial intelligence (AI) and automation tools can enhance Scrum practices by automating routine tasks,

providing predictive analytics for project management, and offering new ways for creative problem-solving.

2. **Virtual and Augmented Reality:**

- Discuss the implications of virtual and augmented reality technologies in Scrum meetings and presentations, enhancing remote collaboration, and offering immersive ways to review and iterate creative work.

3. **Global Collaboration:**

- With the rise of remote work, Scrum teams are becoming more geographically dispersed. Examine tools and strategies for managing global Scrum teams effectively, focusing on overcoming time zone and cultural differences to enhance collaboration.

4. **Personalized Learning and Adaptation:**

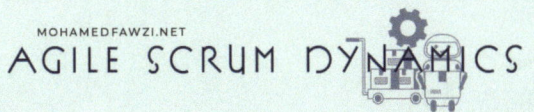

- Look at the role of personalized learning platforms and AI-driven coaching tools in providing tailored training and development opportunities for team members, enabling them to continuously improve their Scrum skills in alignment with project needs.

Preparing for Future Challenges

1. **Handling Increased Complexity:**

   - As projects become more complex and interdisciplinary, creative teams must develop new Scrum methodologies that can handle these complexities without sacrificing agility or creative quality.

2. **Sustaining Innovation:**

   - Identify strategies to maintain a high level of innovation within Scrum frameworks as teams and projects scale. This includes fostering an organizational culture that continually challenges and revisits established Scrum practices to adapt to new creative demands.

3. **Adapting to Rapid Technological Changes:**

- Discuss the need for Scrum frameworks to rapidly integrate new technologies and methodologies to stay relevant and effective in fast-evolving creative industries.

Scrum and Organizational Culture

1. **Embedding Agile Mindsets:**

- Beyond implementing Scrum practices, embedding an agile mindset within the organizational culture is crucial for sustaining success. Explore ways to cultivate this mindset across all levels of an organization.

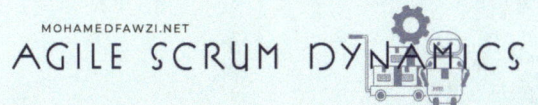

2. **Scrum as a Driver for Change:**

   - Consider how Scrum can act not just as a project management tool, but as a catalyst for broader organizational change, influencing everything from strategic planning to corporate governance.

The future of Scrum in creative fields is promising yet requires vigilance and adaptability. By staying informed about technological advancements and evolving market needs, creative teams can continue to refine their Scrum practices, ensuring they remain both innovative and effective. This chapter sets the stage for creative teams to anticipate and embrace changes, turning potential challenges into opportunities for growth.

Chapter 8
Bringing It All Together

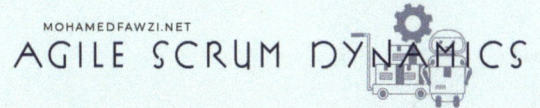

Chapter 8

Bringing It All Together

Implementing and Sustaining Scrum in Creative Teams

This final chapter synthesizes the insights and strategies explored throughout this book, offering a concise roadmap for creative teams ready to adopt or enhance their Scrum practices. Here, we provide practical steps for implementation, discuss long-term sustainment of Scrum methodologies, and encourage a mindset of continuous improvement.

Synthesis of Key Concepts

The journey through the Scrum framework adapted for creative fields has highlighted several key adaptations:

- **Scrum Roles for Creatives**: Tailoring the roles of Product Owner, Scrum Master, and Team Members to fit creative workflows, focusing on flexibility and fluid collaboration.

- **Artifacts and Ceremonies**: Modifying Scrum artifacts and ceremonies to suit the dynamic nature of creative projects, ensuring they foster creativity while maintaining organizational structure.

- **Communication and Collaboration Tools**: Emphasizing the importance of choosing and utilizing tools that enhance communication and collaboration within creative teams.

Actionable Steps for Implementation

To effectively implement Scrum in your creative team, consider the following steps:

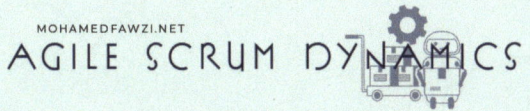

1. **Initial Setup:**

   - **Assess Current Practices:** Start by evaluating your current project management methods to identify strengths and areas for improvement.

   - **Define Scrum Framework:** Customize the Scrum framework to your team's specific needs, considering your creative processes and output.

   - **Team Training:** Ensure that all team members receive thorough training on their roles, the fundamentals of Scrum, and how these will be adapted to your unique environment.

2. **Launching Your First Sprint:**

   - **Sprint Planning:** Conduct a detailed planning session to set clear objectives and deliverables for your first Sprint, ensuring all team members are aligned and understand their tasks.

- **Daily Scrums:** Begin holding daily stand-up meetings to discuss progress, address any issues, and adapt plans as necessary to stay on track.

- **Review and Retrospective:** At the end of the Sprint, hold a review to assess the work completed and conduct a retrospective to discuss what went well and what could be improved.

3. **Refinement and Growth:**

- **Iterative Improvement:** Use insights from Sprint retrospectives to continuously refine your Scrum practices.

- **Scalability:** As your team grows or as projects increase in complexity, adapt and scale your Scrum practices accordingly.

Sustaining Scrum in Creative Environments

Implementing Scrum is just the beginning. Sustaining its practices requires ongoing effort:

- **Foster an Agile Culture:** Cultivate an environment that embraces the agile principles of flexibility, collaboration, and openness to change.

- **Continuous Learning:** Encourage team members to keep up with new Scrum training and developments, which can bring fresh perspectives and practices to your projects.

- **Feedback Mechanisms:** Establish robust channels for continuous feedback, both from within the team and from external stakeholders, to keep improving your processes.

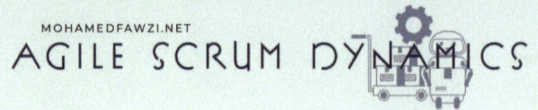

Final Thoughts

Adopting Scrum in creative fields can significantly enhance the way teams manage projects, collaborate, and produce innovative outcomes. As you integrate Scrum into your daily workflows, remember that agility is not just about speed but also about resilience and the ability to adapt to new challenges and opportunities.

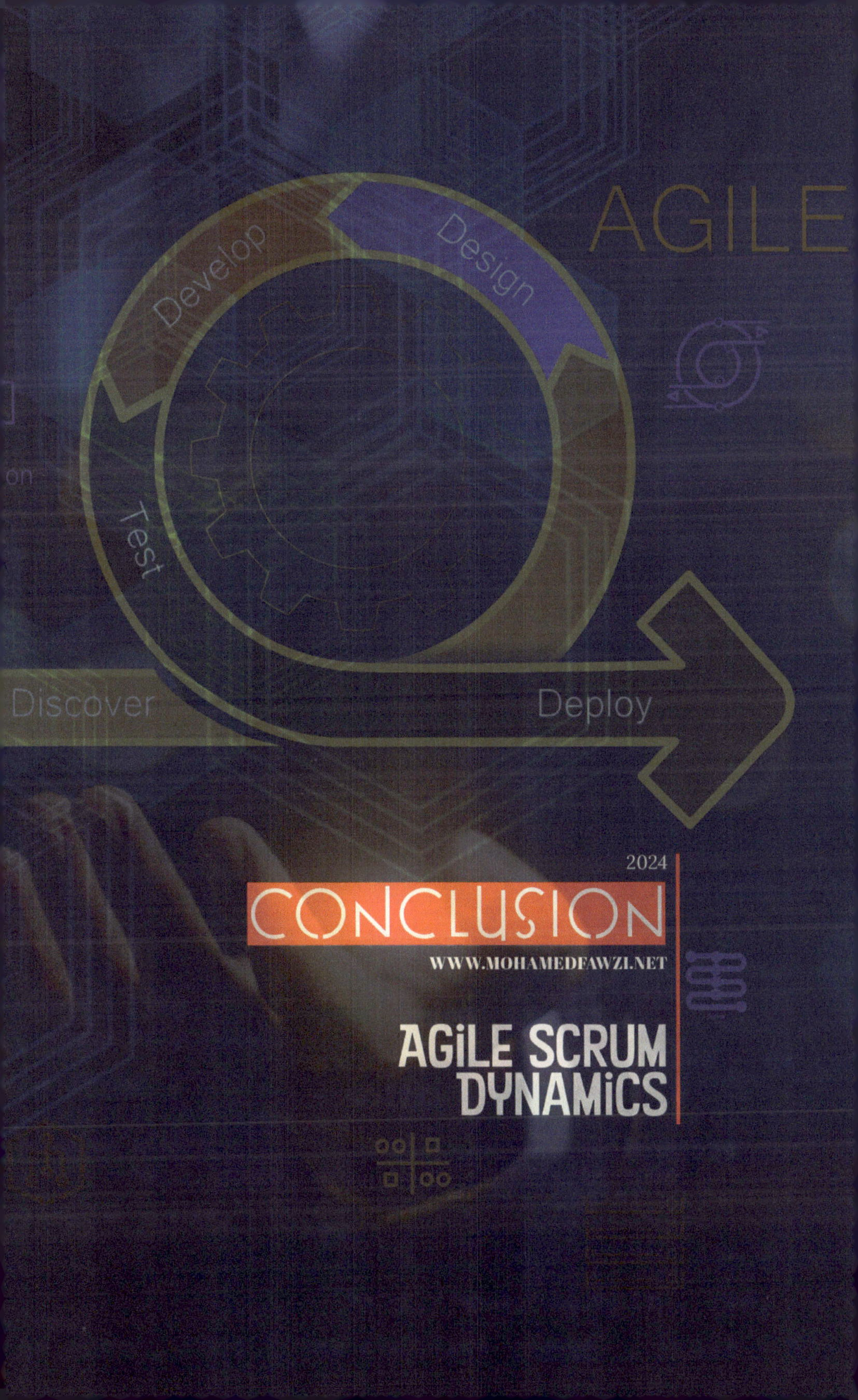

AGILE
Develop
Design
Test
Discover
Deploy
2024
CONCLUSION
WWW.MOHAMEDFAWZI.NET
AGiLE SCRUM
DYNAMiCS

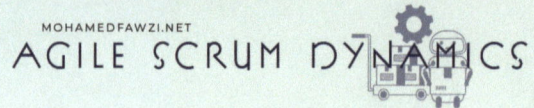

Conclusion

As we close this exploration of Scrum in the context of creative fields, we reflect on the transformative power of integrating this agile methodology into your team's workflow. "Agile Scrum Dynamics" has provided you with a comprehensive toolkit designed not only to introduce Scrum principles but to adapt and apply them in a way that catalyzes creativity and efficiency.

Throughout this book, we've traversed the essentials of Scrum adaptation for creatives—tailoring roles, modifying artifacts, and rethinking ceremonies to better fit the nonlinear, innovative paths that creative projects often take. We've delved into the practical applications of Scrum, equipped with tools and techniques that enhance communication and project management within dynamic environments. Moreover, we've ventured into advanced strategies for sustaining and scaling Scrum practices, ensuring they remain robust and responsive as your projects and teams evolve.

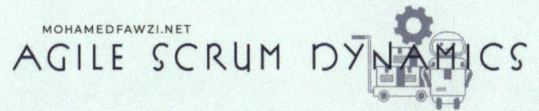

Implementing Scrum in a creative setting is not without its challenges; it requires a shift in mindset from all team members, a commitment to continuous improvement, and an openness to evolving processes. Yet, the rewards—increased productivity, enhanced collaboration, and a more organized approach to innovation—are profound. Scrum offers a framework that not only supports the management of creative projects but also enhances the creative process itself.

As you move forward, remember that Scrum is more than a methodology—it is a journey of ongoing adaptation and learning. Each project presents an opportunity to refine your approach, learn from experiences, and continuously improve your workflows. Embrace these opportunities, encourage your teams to innovate within the Scrum framework, and watch as your projects transform from ideas to impactful creative achievements.

Thank you for joining me on this journey through "Agile Scrum Dynamics." Whether you are a Scrum novice seeking to bring

structure to chaotic creative processes or a seasoned professional looking to refine your approach, I hope this book serves as a valuable resource on your path to mastering Scrum in the creative world. The future of project management in creative fields is agile, and with Scrum, you are well-equipped to lead the charge.

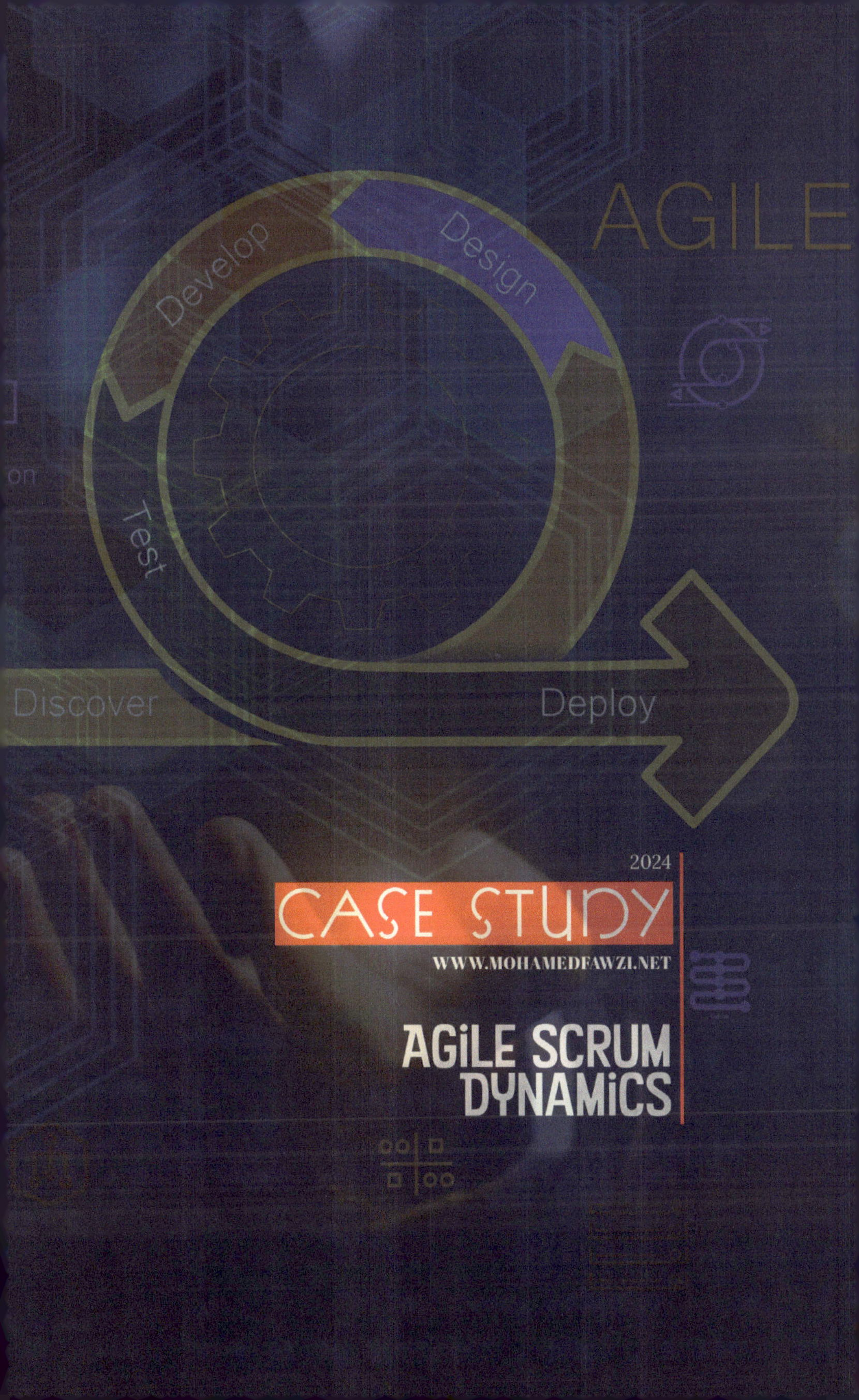

AGILE
Develop
Design
Test
Discover
Deploy
2024
CASE STUDY
WWW.MOHAMEDFAWZI.NET
AGILE SCRUM
DYNAMICS

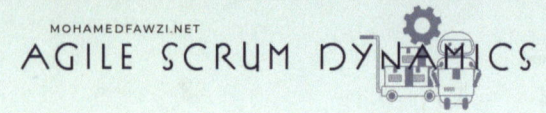

Comprehensive Case Study

ISD Software Solutions

ISD Software Solutions is a technology company specializing in sophisticated software for remote alarms, monitoring, and situational awareness. As the Chief Information Security Officer (CISO) at ISD, I led the initiative to adopt Scrum methodologies across our product development teams. This initiative was aimed at enhancing product management, improving team collaboration, and ensuring that our development practices could keep pace with the rapidly changing technological landscape.

Challenge

Before the adoption of Scrum, our product development process was plagued by slow response times to market changes,

inefficient project management, and siloed department operations. These issues were becoming increasingly detrimental to our ability to innovate and respond effectively to customer needs.

Scrum Implementation

To revolutionize our approach to product development, we implemented the following Scrum methodologies:

1. **Formation of Scrum Teams:**

   - We organized our staff into cross-functional Scrum teams, each encompassing members from different departments including development, operations, and marketing. This approach facilitated diverse input and expertise right from the planning stage of each product.

2. **Scrum Events Adaptation:**

  - **Sprint Planning**: Each sprint began with a thorough planning meeting where teams discussed the goals for the sprint and planned tasks that would align with the overall product roadmap.

  - **Daily Stand-ups**: Short daily meetings were held to keep the team aligned on progress, identify any blockers, and adjust plans swiftly to ensure continuous progress.

  - **Sprint Reviews**: At the end of each sprint, the team reviewed completed work, demonstrating new features to stakeholders to gather feedback and adjust the product direction as needed.

  - **Retrospectives**: These meetings were used to reflect on the sprint process, discussing what went well and what could be improved, fostering a culture of continuous improvement.

3. **Product Backlog Management**:

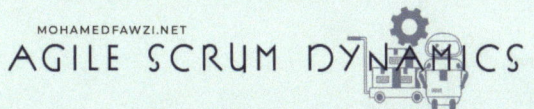

- The Product Owner maintained a prioritized backlog that was regularly refined and adjusted based on stakeholder feedback and market trends. This ensured that the team always worked on the most valuable tasks.

Overcoming Challenges

Adopting Scrum was initially challenging due to resistance from team members accustomed to traditional project management methods. To address this, we implemented several key strategies:

- **Comprehensive Training**: Conducted extensive training sessions to ensure all team members understood the principles of Scrum and how these principles would be applied to their work.

- **Gradual Rollout**: We started with pilot projects, allowing teams to gradually adapt to the new workflows and see the benefits of Scrum firsthand before a full-scale implementation.

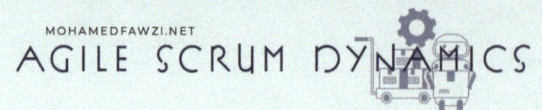

- **Regular Feedback Loops:** Instituted regular feedback sessions to hear concerns and adapt the implementation strategy accordingly, ensuring buy-in from all levels of the organization.

Outcomes

The shift to Scrum methodologies significantly transformed our product management approach by:

- **Increasing Flexibility:** Our teams became more agile, able to adjust plans quickly based on real-time feedback and changes in the market.

- **Enhancing Collaboration:** Cross-functional teams fostered a collaborative environment where different perspectives were valued, leading to more innovative solutions.

- **Improving Product Quality and Customer Satisfaction**: Continuous integration of customer feedback into the

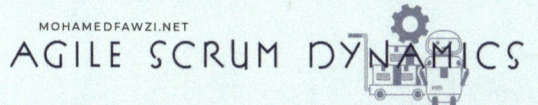

development process ensured that the final products were closely aligned with user needs.

Conclusion

The adoption of Scrum methodologies at ISD Software Solutions has not only improved our product development lifecycle but also created a more dynamic and responsive culture. By embedding Scrum across our teams, we have been able to enhance innovation, streamline processes, and deliver products that truly meet the evolving demands of our customers. As we move forward, Scrum will continue to be a central pillar in our strategy to lead and innovate in our industry.

Develop

Design

Test

Discover

Deploy

AUTHOR
WWW.MOHAMEDFAWZI.NET
2024

AGILE SCRUM DYNAMICS

me@mohamedfawzi.net
Dubai, UAE

Mohamed Fawzi Elgendi

AI Enthusiast & Mental wellness Author

Pioneering Digital Innovation, AI Advancement, Information Security, and Promoting Mental Wellness.

400+ Mentee
70+ Project
17+ Book
16Y+ Experience

Chief Information Security Officer (CISO)

Chief Digital and AI Officer (CDAO)

Post Graduate Program in Artificial Intelligence For Leaders

Bachelor's degree in Computer and Systems Engineering

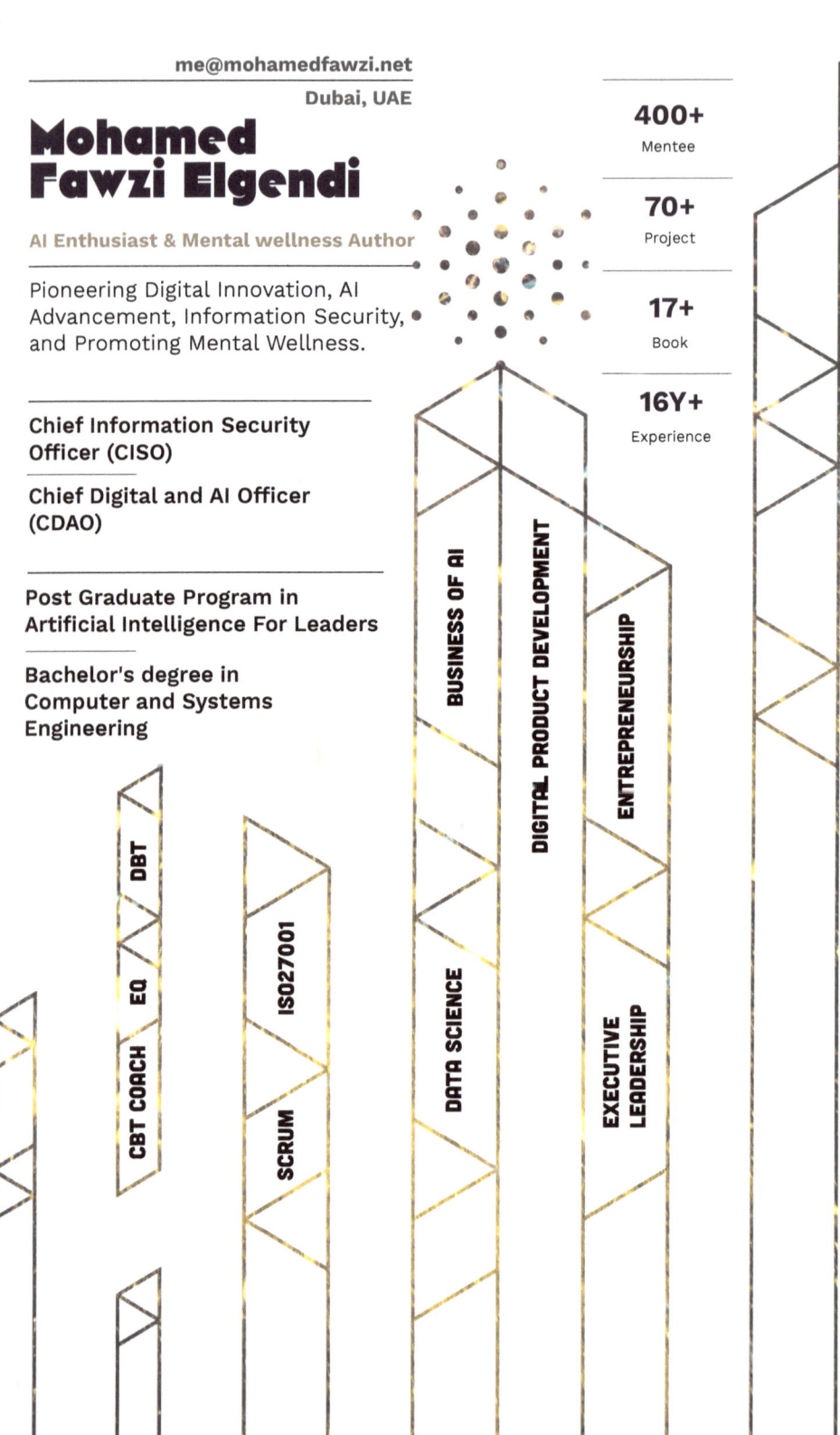

- DBT
- EQ
- CBT COACH
- ISO27001
- SCRUM
- BUSINESS OF AI
- DATA SCIENCE
- DIGITAL PRODUCT DEVELOPMENT
- ENTREPRENEURSHIP
- EXECUTIVE LEADERSHIP

www.ingramcontent.com/pod-product-compliance
Lightning Source LLC
Chambersburg PA
CBHW040228220526
45473CB00001B/165